DATE DUE

4/23/09			

The COIN Counting Book

by Rozanne Lanczak Williams

Charlesbridge

A quarter, a dime,
A nickel, one cent.
Let's count all our coins
Before they get spent.

For Cris, Christiana, Adam and Laura too.
For my fun family, this one's for you.
— R.L.W.

Published by Charlesbridge
85 Main Street, Watertown, MA 02472
(617) 926-0329 • www.charlesbridge.com

Printed in Korea
(hc) 10 9 8 7 6 5
(sc) 10 9 8

Library of Congress Cataloging-in-Publication Data
Williams, Rozanne Lanczak.
The coin counting book/Rozanne L. Williams.
p.   cm.
ISBN-13: 978-0-88106-325-7; ISBN-10: 0-88106-325-8 (reinforced for library use)
ISBN-13: 978-0-88106-326-4; ISBN-10: 0-88106-326-6 (softcover)
1. Counting—Juvenile literature. 2. Coins, American—
Juvenile literature. [1. Counting. 2. Coins.] I. Title.
QA113.W58   2001
513.2'11—dc21   00-047394

Display type and text type set in Incised 901 BT
Color separations by Sung In Printing, South Korea
Printed and bound by Sung In Printing, South Korea
Production supervision by Brian G. Walker
Designed by Diane M. Earley

One penny, two pennies,
Three pennies, four.
What will we get
When we add just one more?

one penny + one penny + one penny + one penny + one penny = one nickel

1¢ + 1¢ + 1¢ + 1¢ + 1¢ = 5¢

One nickel

Let's count our five pennies
Just one more time.
If we add five *more* pennies
We'll have . . .

one penny + one penny + one penny + one penny + one penny +

1¢ + 1¢ + 1¢ + 1¢ + 1¢ +

one penny + one penny + one penny + one penny + one penny = one dime

1¢ + 1¢ + 1¢ + 1¢ + 1¢ = 10¢

One dime

What else equals
A dime or ten cents?
Five pennies and one nickel—
Makes perfect math sense.

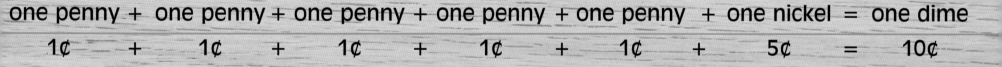

one penny + one penny + one penny + one penny + one penny + one nickel = one dime

1¢ + 1¢ + 1¢ + 1¢ + 1¢ + 5¢ = 10¢

There's one more way
To make a dime.
Put down two nickels,
One at a time.

one nickel   +   one nickel   =   one dime

5¢   +   5¢   =   10¢

Look! Lots of pennies!
Can you count twenty-five?

5 pennies   +   5 pennies   +   5 pennies

5¢   +   5¢   +   5¢

But it's faster,
It's quicker,
If we count them by fives.
5, 10, 15, 20, 25

+   5 pennies   +   5 pennies   =   twenty-five pennies

+   5¢   +   5¢   =   25¢

Twenty-five pennies!
We might drop a few.
We have too many pennies.
What can we do?

We can trade for one **quarter**, shiny and new.

One **quarter**

Two dimes and a nickel
Make one quarter, too.
So do five nickels,
Five nickels for you!

one dime + one dime + one nickel = one quarter

10¢ + 10¢ + 5¢ = 25¢

Let's trade all our coins,
Our nickels and dimes.
Quarters are better.
They save counting time.

one nickel + one nickel + one nickel + one nickel + one nickel = one quarter

5¢ + 5¢ + 5¢ + 5¢ + 5¢ = 25¢

What can we do
With two quarters, my friend?
We can trade both of them
For one coin to spend.

Fifty cents.

There are many ways
To make this amount.
Let's jump right in,
And start to count.

one quarter + one quarter = one half-dollar

25¢ + 25¢ = 50¢

one dime + one dime + one dime + one dime + one dime = one half-dollar

10¢ + 10¢ + 10¢ + 10¢ + 10¢ = 50¢

one nickel + one nickel + one nickel + one nickel + one nickel +

5¢ + 5¢ + 5¢ + 5¢ + 5¢ +

one nickel + one nickel + one nickel + one nickel + one nickel = one half-dollar

5¢ + 5¢ + 5¢ + 5¢ + 5¢ = 50¢

We have lots of coins.
We have so many.
Can we trade them in
For some money less heavy?

How about a **dollar**?

What makes a dollar?
Let's count pennies by tens.

10 pennies + 10 pennies + 10 pennies + 10 pennies + 10 pennies +

10¢ + 10¢ + 10¢ + 10¢ + 10¢ +

It's fun counting pennies—Let's count them again!
10, 20, 30, 40, 50, 60, 70, 80, 90, 100

10 pennies + 10 pennies + 10 pennies + 10 pennies + 10 pennies = one dollar

10¢ + 10¢ + 10¢ + 10¢ + 10¢ = $1.00

What else makes one dollar?
It's important to know.

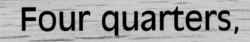

Four quarters,

Spread out our coins.
Let's have a coin show!

Twenty nickels,

Ten dimes in a row.

Let's count out dollars—

Ready,

20 nickels = one dollar   10 dimes = one dollar

Set,   *Go!*

4 quarters = one dollar   2 half dollars = one dollar

We've counted our money,
Lots for me and for you.
Our pockets are full!
Now what do we do?

Let's see . . .
Well, that all depends . . .
If we save *some* of it—
The rest we can spend!

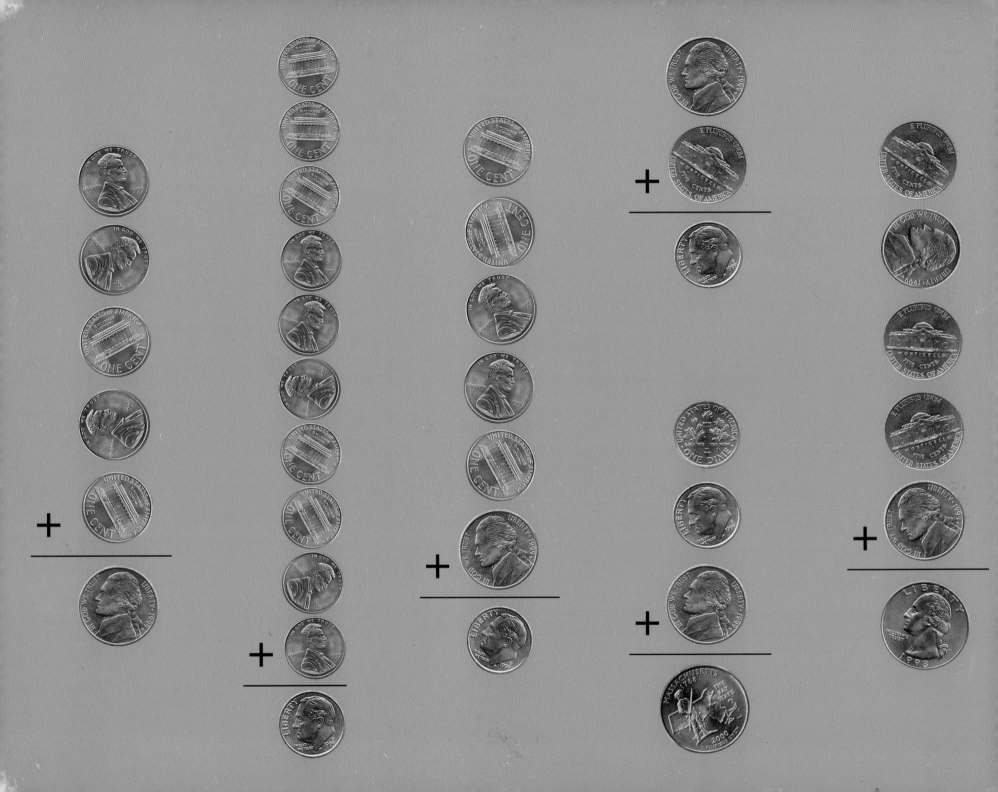

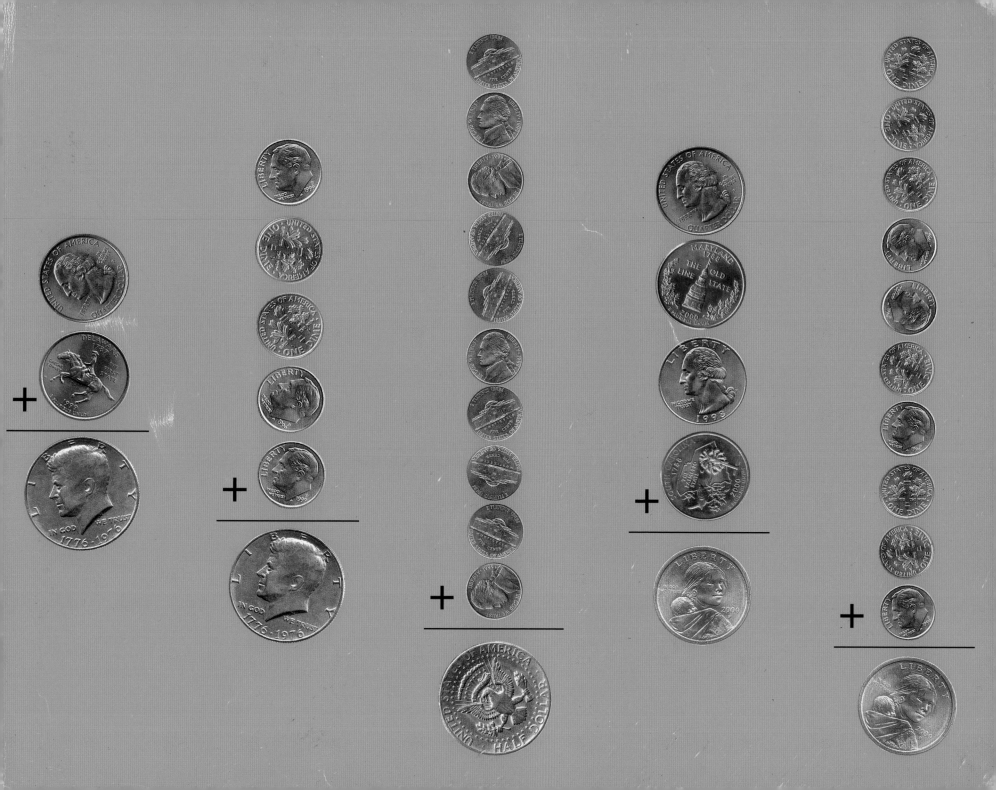